or before

Life With Loopy

First published in Great Britain by
HarperCollins Publishers Ltd in 1992
First published in Picture Lions in 1993
Picture Lions is an imprint of the Children's Division,
part of HarperCollins Publishers Limited,
77-85 Fulham Palace Road, Hammersmith,
London W6 8JB
Reprinted 1993

Printed in Hong Kong

This book is set in 24/38 Bookman Italic

Life With Loopy

Libby Butterworth
Illustrated by Siobhan Dodds

PictureLions
An Imprint of HarperCollinsPublishers

Loopy is a mad dog

and sometimes a sad dog

or even a glad dog

and occasionally a bad dog.

Loopy is a black and white dog

not a red

or blue

or brown dog.

Loopy is a spotty dog

no stars

nor stripes

and definitely not a mottled dog.

Loopy is a running dog

a let's-lie-in-the-sun dog

a never-late-for-dinner dog

a having lots of fun dog.

Sometimes she's a dreaming dog

then she's definitely a top dog

a leader of the pack dog

a winner-of-awards dog.

She pretends that she's a sheep dog

or even a police dog

a brave and fearless rescue dog

but really – she's just my dog.

Loopy is not a fighting dog

but a let's-look-for-a-stick dog

a bury-a-bone-a-day dog

a run-away-and-hide dog.

She really is a messy dog

a jump-out-of-the-bath dog

but such a waggly-tail dog

she's just about the best dog!

Here are some more Picture Lions

for you to enjoy.